TURNER SECOND YEAR MCQ

OBJECTIVE QUESTION ANSWERS

MANOJ DOLE

Digitization is the need of the time. In the future, training in industrial training institutes will need to be conducted using online internet to make training more convenient and easy. E-books containing a set of MCQ questions will be made available to the trainees as they need to be more accustomed to the multiple choice questions MCQ to prepare for the online exams taking place in their industrial training institutes.

With all these factors in mind, Mr. Manoj Madhukar Dole Instructor, Industrial Training Institute, Satara, has written books according to the new annual system and NSQF-5 syllabus. And they've created theoretical mobile apps and blogs to make training easier, and made all these educational materials available for download on the world famous websites Google Play Store, Amazon and Apple Book Store.

The books were published by Hon'ble Joint Director Shri Rajendra Ghume Saheb Regional Office of Vocational Education and Training, Pune on 9/1/2019, at this time Shri Prakash Saigavkar Saheb Principal Government Industrial Training Institute Aundh Pune, Shri Tukaram Misal Saheb Principal Govt. Q. Sanstha Satara, Shri Sachin Dhumal Saheb District Vocational Education and Training Officer Satara, Shri Yatin Pargaonkar Saheb Principal Govt. Q. Sanstha Kolhapur, Shri Vikas Teke Saheb Inspector Vocational Education and Training Regional Office Pune, Palekar Foods Products Pvt. Ltd. Entrepreneurial Chairman of Satara Mr. Nilkanthrao Palekar Saheb, Chairman of Hira Foods Mr. Ibrahim Baba Tamboli Saheb, Mrs. Shalmali Pawar Headmaster Government Technical School Center Satara and other dignitaries were present on the occasion.

Contents

Prologue

Turner Second Year MCQ is a simple e-Book for ITI Engineering Course Turner, Second Year, Sem- 3 & 4, Revised NSQF-5 Syllabus in 2022, It contains objective questions with underlined & bold correct answers MCQ covering all topics including all about The machining of different irregular shaped job using different lathe accessories, different utility items viz., Crank Shaft (single throw), Stub arbor, components (male & female) by performing different turning activities, CNC operations, operating the CNC turn centre to produce components, multi-media based CNC simulated and on actual intermediate production based CNC machine, special operation on lathe viz., worm shaft cutting, different engineering components viz., drill chuck, collet chuck, screw jack, box nut and lots more.

We add new question answers with each new version. Please email us in case of any errors/omissions. This is arguably the largest and best e-Book for All engineering multiple choice questions and answers.

As a student you can use it for your exam prep. This e-Book is also useful for professors to refresh material.

Foreword

Vocational education and training is imparted through the Department of Vocational Education and Training through the Department of Business Education and Business Practical to supply multi-skilled artisans in line with the rapidly growing demand in the industrial sector in the 21st century. All the occupations within the institutions are important, as the trainees from these occupations develop multi-skills as per the demands of the industry.

with the noble intention of making available MCQ e-books suitable for all businesses, considering that all the examinations in all the industries in the industrial sector are conducted online and include MCQ method questions. Mr. Manoj Madhukar Dole has written a very good e-book on MCQ method as per the new annual syllabus. This e-book will definitely be a guide for all the trainees, trainee candidates, training instructors and others concerned.

The author of the book is Mr. Manoj Madhukar Dole, Instructor Gov. ITI Satara has 17 years of training experience. Written as a new annual pattern, this e-book incorporates modern digital QR Code technology to understand the layout, simple language, and simple syntax, diagrams and videos for each subject. So I am sure that this e-book will definitely be useful for in-depth study and exam practice. The work they have done is certainly commendable.

Mr. Tukaram Misal
Principal Government Industrial Training Institute Satara.

Preface

DGET New Delhi and CSTARI Kolkata have been implementing an annual pattern for all businesses in ITI since the August 2018 session. The examination system will also be changed and it will be online from this year and since all the questions are of Objective Type (MCQ), the trainees are in dire need of in-depth study. It is with this in mind that we are delighted to present the books based on the old NIMI pattern and a complete overview of the new annual pattern, and we hope that these books will be a guide for all business directors and trainees. Is.

For writing these books, Johar Awate Saheb, Principal of ITI Akluj. Former Principal of ITI Satara Saigavkar Saheb, Assistant Director Shri Chandrakant Dhekne Saheb Regional Office of Vocational Education and Training, Pune, District Vocational Education and Training Officer Sachin Dhumal Saheb and Headmaster Government Technical School Kendra Shalmali Pawar Madam and son Adhiraj Dole, mother Kusum Dole, I am very grateful to my father Madhukar Dole and wife Ashwini Dole for their special guidance and cooperation from time to time.

Also, in a very short period of time, the book was reviewed by Shri Rajendra Ghume Saheb, Joint Director, Vocational Education and Training Regional Office, Pune, for his invaluable time in publishing the book. I am sincerely grateful for their feedback.

I am grateful to the Instructor of ITI Satara for there continuous support from the very beginning of writing the book.

From this book, I consider myself blessed to have shared my thoughts on e-learning with you. I will not claim that this book is perfect, because considering the perfection, this book is an attempt and is in its infancy. They will be valuable for improvement if they are tested and suggested.

Manoj Dole
Dated 9/1/2019

Acknowledgements

The industrial training and theoretical examination system of our industrial training institutes and these changes have been accepted by the craft instructors and the trainees. Theoretical examinations conducted in your industrial training institutes are also conducted online. Since these examinations are of multiple choice MCQ method, the trainees will need to get more practice of such questions.

With all these considerations in mind, Mr. Manoj Madhukar, Director, Dole Crafts, Katari Industrial Training Institute, Satara, has done a thorough study and with his diligent work and added his keen intellect, according to the new annual system and NSQF-5 syllabus, e-book of Katari and other machine trades. -Book) and they have created mobile apps and blogs on theoretical topics to make training easier and have made all these educational materials available for download on the world famous websites Google Play Store, Amazon and Apple Book Store. Training has been made easier by creating a print version and using advanced techniques like QR Code.

All these educational materials will definitely be a guide for all the trainees for in-depth study and for the craft instructors and other concerned who are imparting vocational training.

CHAPTER ONE

Turner Second Year MCQ Drawings

Online Test Exam

ITI Books

CNC Course

AutoCAD CAM

JOB & Apprentice

Online Theory

Computer Course

Trading Course

Web Designing

MSCIT Course

Shopping Business

Internet Business

Remotasks Course

Online Services

Top Sportsmans

Indian Army

Freedom Fighters

Top Scientists

Social Reformers

Motivational Speaker

Top Richest People

Join WhatsApp Group

Join Facebook Group

Like Facebook Page

PAN / Adhar / Licence
Passport

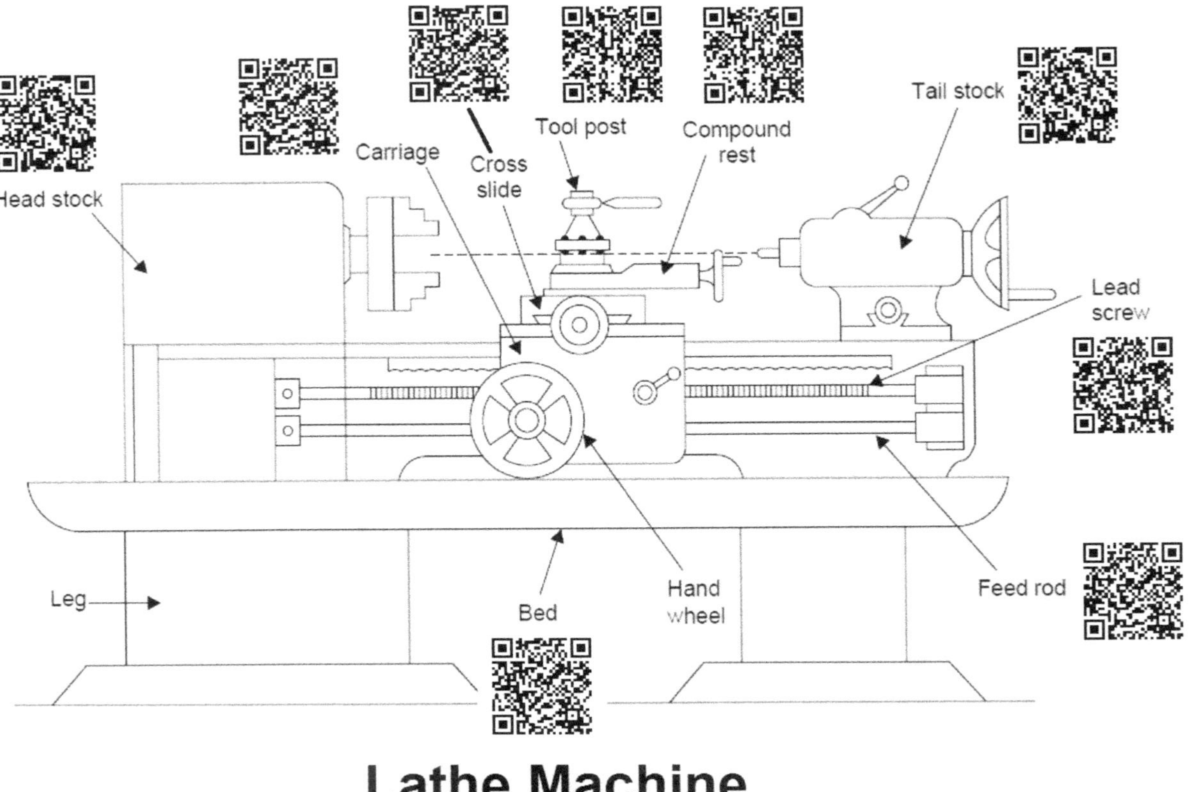

Lathe machine

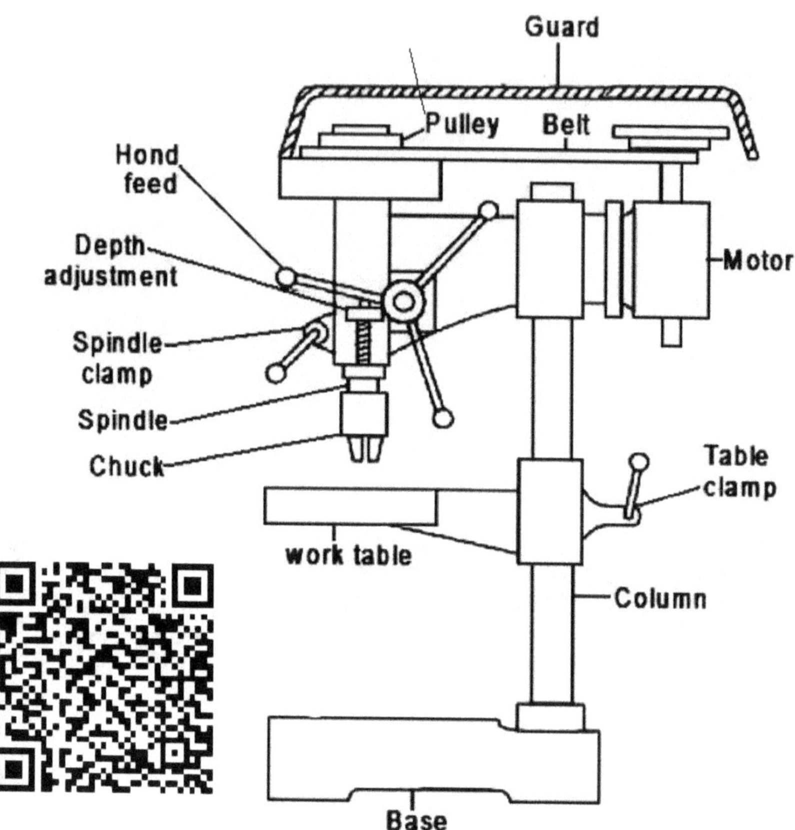

Piller Drilling Machine

Drilling machine

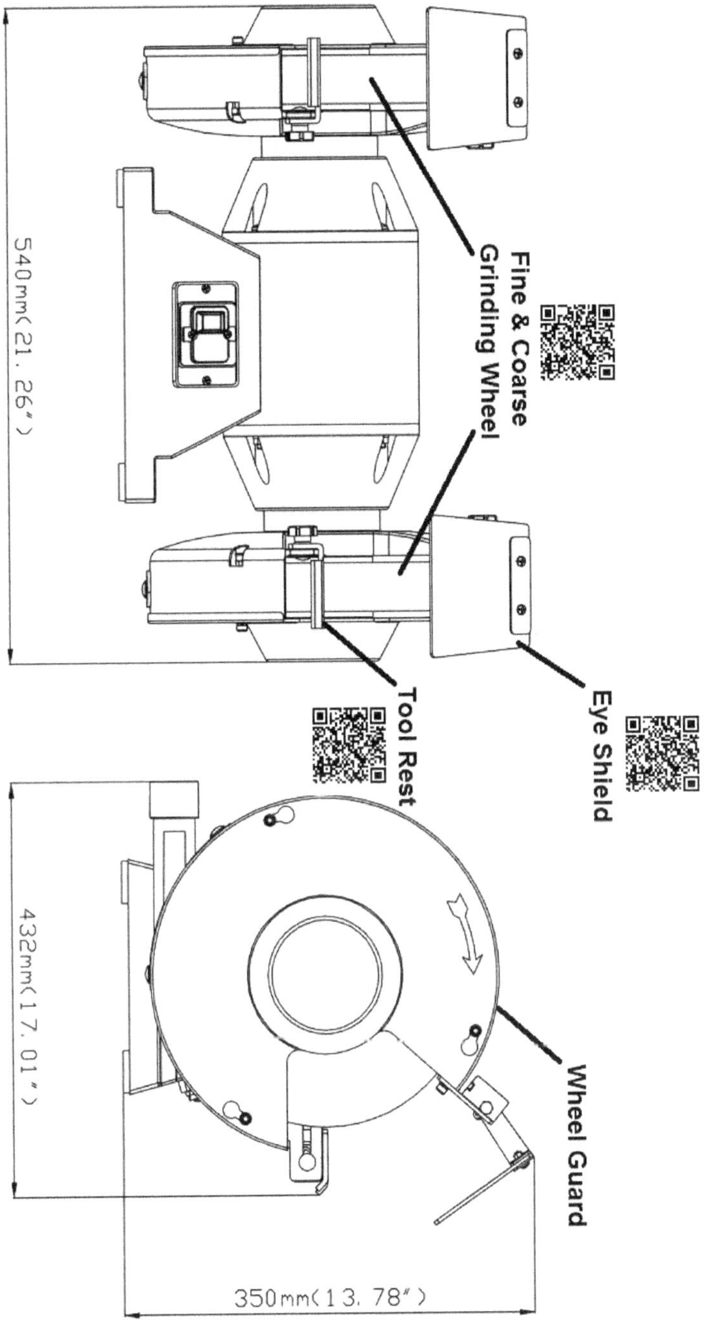

Bench Grinding Machine

bench grinding machine

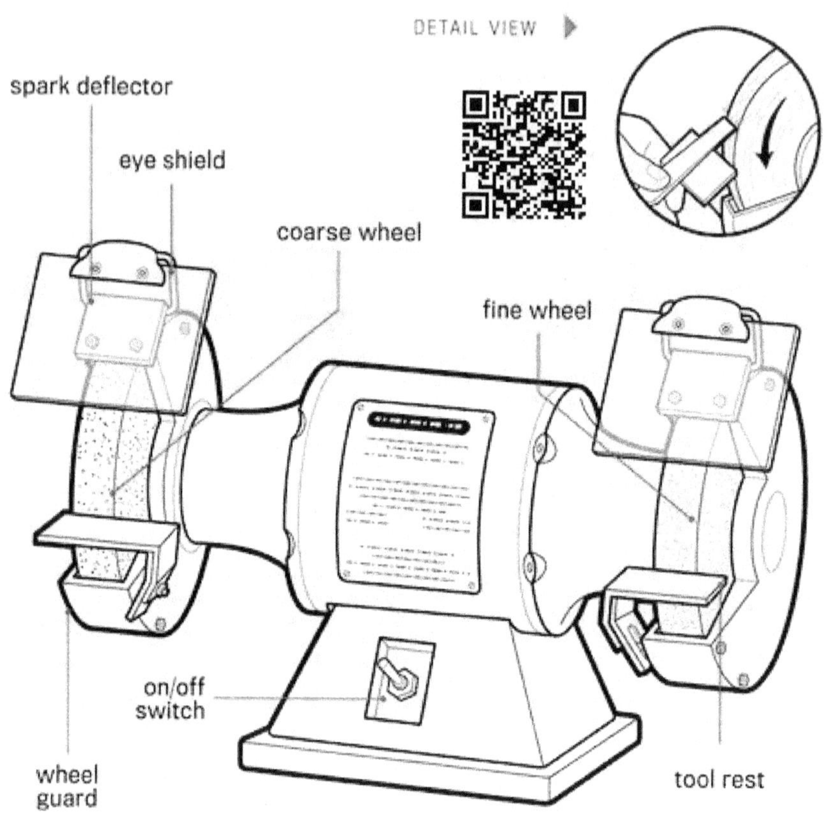

bench grinding machine

CHAPTER TWO

Turner Second Year MCQ

1] How many types of Lathe as per manufacturing?

A] Two

B] Three

C] Four

D] Five

2] How many types of Centre Lathe?

A] Two

B] Three

C] Four

D] Five

<u>Lathe Machine Animation & Video</u>

3] How many types of production lathe?

A] Two

B] Three

C] Four

D] Five

4] Which type of lathe is Roller Lathe?

A] Bench Lathe

B] Special Lathe

C] Production Lathe

D] Centre Lathe

Lathe machine Animation & Video

5] For mass-production which machine is used?

A] Centre Lathe

B] Production Lathe

C] Special Lathe

D] Engine Lathe

6] Which lathe is used for more accurate job?

A] Centre Lathe
B] Special Lathe
C] Production Lathe
D] Tool Room Lathe
7] The accuracy of Tool Room Lathe is...] to Compeer Centre Lathe.]
(A] Less
(B] More
(C] Very Less
(D] Equal
8] In Locomotive Assemble Wheel with Axel is turning on ......Lathe
(A] Centre Lathe
(B] Tool Room Lathe
(C] Wheel Lathe
(D] Gap Bed Lathe
9] Cast iron is used for manufacturing machine beds because -------
A] it can resist more compressive stress
B] it is heavy in weight
C] It is cheaper metal
D] It is a brittle metal
10] Which one of the following operations can't be performed on a Center Lathe?]
A] Turning
B] Thread cutting
C] Gear cutting
D] Taper turning

Gear Animation & Video

11] While turning on M.S] job which types of good chips produce from cutting tool & material?
A] Spiral chips
B] circular chips
C] long chips
D] straight & long chips
12] Cemented carbide material is....?
A] Ferrous metal
B] non-ferrous metal
C] alloy steel
D] non-ferrous alloy
13] For carbide tip tool turning on hard material it has.....ecential?

A] Side Rake angle

B] Zero Rake angle

C] Positive Rake angle

D] <u>Negative Rake angle</u>

14] A slot is to be milled in a steel component using a 9 mm diameter slot mill rotating at 373 rpm] The cutting speed will be

A] <u>10.55 m/min</u>

B] 26.7 m/min

C] 181.9 m/min

D] 11 m/min

15] A 12 mm diameter end mill is to be set for a cutting speed of 14 m/min] the r.p.m] to be set on the machine should be

A] 271.7 rpm

B] 183.17 rpm

C] 76 rpm

D] <u>371.21 rpm</u>

16] A cutter has a diameter of 80 mm] if the cutting speed is to be 20 m/min] the rpm of the spindle should be

A] 90.7 rpm

B] <u>79.55 rpm</u>

C] 25.75 rpm

D] 107.95 rpm

17] Zero Rake angle give for tool?

A] To avoid friction of tool

B] <u>For increase tool life</u>

C] For increase straight of tool

D] For better finishing on job

18] ....] & ....] Shape job turning in form turning?

A] Plain & V] Shape

B] Squre & Round

C] <u>Concave & Convex</u>

D] V & Round

19] Which part making by form turning of machine?

A] Base

B] Bed

C] Carrage

D] <u>Handles</u>

20] Form turning done for this purpose....?

A] <u>For attractive job</u>
B] for large material cutting
C] for better finishing
D] for smallest cut on job
21] Which type of metal tool use for mass production of form turning?
A] H.S.S]
B] H.C.S]
C] <u>Carbide</u>
D] Cementite
22] What is template?
A] One of the cutting operation
B] One of the form turning
C] <u>same figure of the job</u>
D] one of the tool
23] Which purpose use template?
A] <u>For marking & checking</u>
B] for threading
C] for turning
D] for measuring
24] Which material is use for making template?
A] H.C.S] plate
B] Special tool steel
C] brass or copper
d] <u>G.I] sheet or M.S] thin sheet</u>
25] ---------------is used for checking shape of component
<u>A] Template</u>
B] Snap gauge
C] Instrument
D] Sine bar
26] The dial test indicator shows the measurement as.....
A] the actual size of the component
B] the difference between the two steps of 5 mm
<u>C] the magnified small variations in sizes throut a pointer</u>
D] the direct reading of the dimension
27] The principle of working of the dial test indicator is
A the linear motion is converted into reciprocating motion using slotted link

B the linear motion is converted into rotary motion using rack and pinion

C magnifications of small variation using lenses

D magnifications by electronic means:

28] Which of the following instrument is used to check the concentricity of the outside diameter...?

A] Outside micrometer

B] Dial test indicator

C] Vernier caliper

D] Dial caliper

Dial test indicator Animation & Video

29] Which one of the following mechanism is used to convert the linear motion of the plunger of a dial test indicator to the rotary motion of the pointer....?

A] Screw thread mechanism

B] Quick Return mechanism

C] Rack and pinion mechanism

D] Hydraulic mechanism

30] To check the dimensional accuracy of identical components a dial test indicator is set to the size and used as a comparator what will you use to set the dial quage...?

A] Snap guage

B] Outside micrometer

C] Sine Bar

D] Slip guage

31] The use of dial test indicator..?

A] to check to length of blind hole to an accuracy of 0.01 mm

B] to check the external diameter to on accuracy of 0.001 mm

C] to check the cylindricity of turned job to an accuracy of 0.01 mm

D] None of the above

32] Dial test indicator is used..?

A] To check the concentricily of holes

B] to check the cylindricity of shaft

C] to check the parallelism of job to an accuracy 0.01 mm

D] All of the above

33] In the liver type dial test indicator the magnification of movement is abtained by this mechanism...?

A] Rack and pinion

B] <u>Lever and scroll</u>

C] Screw thread

D] Quick return

34] Dial test indicator shows measurement...?

A] Actual size of job

B] difference between two steps by 0.5 mm

C] Direct reading of size

D] <u>Small variation in the size by pointer</u>

35]To check the dimensional accuracy of identical components, a dial test indicator is set-for t 6 Size and used as a comparator] What will you use to set to the dial test indicator?

A] Dial test indicator

B] Teeter gauge

C] <u>Slip gauge</u>

D], surface gauge

36] Uses of a dial test indicator are ----------

A] To check plane surface for parallelism and flatness

B] To check the straightness of shaft and bars

C] To check concentricity of holes and shafts

D] <u>All the above</u>

37] The dial test indicators shows that the measurement as -------

A] <u>The magnified small variation is size through a point</u>

B] The difference between the top steps of the 5 mm

C] The actual size of the component

D] The direct reading of the dimension

38] Name the instrument which magnifies the small variation is size measured]

A] Vernier calliper

B] Micrometer

C] <u>Dial indicator</u>

D] Steel rule

39] Which one of the following is not correct about dial test indicator?

A] It has 100 divisions on its dial

B] Motion of the stem is transferred to the dial through Gear train

C] <u>Its accuracy is 0.1 mm</u>

D] Used in conjunction with depth gauge

40] in following drawing, which of the front clearance angel?

A] <u>Front clearance angle</u>

B] Wedge angle

C] Cutting angle

D] Back rake angle

41] When cutting tool start his action & cutting force in increase at this position subsequent effect of tool is..?

A] Clearance angle of tool is high

B] <u>Clearance angle of tool is low</u>

C] Rake angle of tool is low

D] Rake angle of tool is high

42] The purpose of Rake angle for tool is?

A] <u>Right direction for mental chips</u>

B] Good finishing on job

C] For increase life of tool

D] For avoid friction in between job & tool

43] The purpose of provide clearance angle for cutting tool is?

A] For right direction of metal cutting chips

B] reduce friction on hit of job

C] <u>for sage of job friction</u>

D] for better finishing on job

44] If cutting tools setting upper centre height done what happen?

A] <u>Encrease top Rake angle</u>

B] less top Rake angle

C] No effect on Top Rake angle

D] Encrease clearance angle

45] What happen if cutting tool setting done lower of center height?

A] Encrease top Rake angle

B] <u>Decrease top Rake angle</u>

C] No any effect on to Rake

D] Decrease clearance angle

46] If cutting tool is upsetting of centre of job?

A] Encrease front clearance angle

B] <u>Decrease front clearance angle</u>

C] no any effect on front clearance angle

D] none of them

47] If cutting tool is down setting of centre of job?

A] <u>Front clearance angle is increase</u>

B] Front clearance angle is decrease

C] No any effect on clearance angle

D] None of them

48] Zero Rake angle give for tool?

A] To avoid friction of tool

B] <u>For increase tool life</u>

C] For increase straight of tool

D] For better finishing on job

49] For carbide tip tool turning on hard material it has.....ecential?

A] Side Rake angle

B] Zero Rake angle

C] Positive Rake angle

D] <u>Negative Rake angle</u>

50] For do not break cutting edge of cutting tool...?

A] Feed increase

B] Cutting speed done low

C] Length of nose decrease

D] <u>Use negative rake angle</u>

51] The jig bush used for drilling and reaming of a hole is...?

A] Press fit bush

B] Liner bush

C] <u>Slip renewable bush</u>

D] Fixed renewable bush

52] The following given which device is used for holding job & guide for toll while working?

A] Gauge

B] Housing

C] <u>Jig</u>

D] Fixture

53] The following given device which one for used clamping job only?

A] Jig

B] <u>Fixture</u>

C] Housing

D] Gauge

54] While fabricated by welding job which device is used for holding fixed or revolving if necessary up to 360°C of welding job?

A] Gauge

b] Template

C] Jig

D] <u>Fixture</u>

55] The main things of drilling jig its not clamping with machine table which reason is correct given following?

A] it is strong for operation

B] it is easy for operation

C] many different size holes produce by different setting while drilling on job

D] for this device has lot of time

56] Following which locations is most usefull for round shape job location?

A] pin type locator

B] wedge type locator

C] vee locator

D] adjustable stop locators

57] Following which reason is correct for using bushing in drilling jigs?

A] easy for drilling

B] for fixed drill hole size

C] for accurate drilling operation

D] for given better finish drilling hole

58] The metal for manufacturing jig bush is...?

A] mild steel

B] cast iron

C] cast steel

D] tool steel

59] Given following bush which busing used for locating renewable bushing?

A] press fit bushing

B] linear bushing

C] special bushing

D] knurd bushing

60] jig has tolerance..?

A] five present of job tolerance

B] ten percent of job tolerance

C] 20% to 50% of job tolerance

D] 100% of job tolerance

61] Following which jig is use for location from bore?

A] plate jig

B] solid jig

C] post jig

D] box jig

62] Following which jig having drill plate?

A] solid jig

<u>B] plate jig</u>

C] box jig

D] table jig

63] Following which locator is used for internal diameter location?

A] solid saports

<u>B] Pin type locator</u>

C] Vee locator

D] nest locator

64] Drm jig bushing-are generally hardened to ------------]

A] Mild steel

B] Cast iron

C] Cast steel

<u>D] Tooi steel</u>

65] Jigs is device which -------------

A] Locate the work piece

B] Holding and supporting the work piece

C] Guide the cutting tool

<u>D] Does all the above</u>

66] Which among the following jigs is used forllocation from a bore?

A] Plate jig

B] Solid jig

<u>C] Post jig</u>

D] Box jig

67] Fixture is a production device which -----------]

<u>A] Holds and locate the work piece</u>

B] Holds the piece

C] Chats the work piece,

D] Neither holds nor] Locates the-work piece

68] Which one of the following is used to guide tool and hold the job in mass production? '

A] Gauge]

B] Housing

<u>C] Fixture</u>

D] Jig

69] Which among the following is the purpose for proi/iding bushing in a drill jig?

A] For locating accurately and guiding the drill for precise drilling operation

B] For determining the size of the hole to be drilled

C] For easy drilling

D] For getting good finished surface in the drilled holes

70] Drill jig are used for? _ ,

A] Drill operations only]

B] Clamping the job for drilling

C] Drilling, Reaming, Tapping and other operations

D] Guiding the tools only

71] Which one of the following jigs consists of drill plate, which rests on the component to be drilled?]]]]

A] Solid jig]

B] Plate jig]

C] Box jig

D] Trunnion jig

72] Jig is a device which -----------

A] Locates the work piece]

B] Hold and supports the work piece and guides tool

C] Guides the cutting tool

D] Hold the cutting tool]

73] Drill jig are used for ....]

A] Drilling, reaming, tapping and other allied operations

B] Drilling operations only

C] Clamping the job when drilling

D] Guiding the tool only

74] Fixture is a production device which---------: -----

A] holds the work piece '

B] Locate the work piece

C] Holds and locates the work piece

D] Neither holds nor locates the work piece

75] Purpose of the Box Jig is to

A] Hold the job and guide the tool to produce internal threads

B] To produce many inclined holes

C] To produce many straight holes

D] None of these

76] Jigs and fixtures are --------]
A] Machining tools
B] Precision tools
C] Both (a] & (b]
D] None of these
77] 'How jig are in terms of weight compared to fixtures?
A] Jigs are lighter than fixtures
B] Jigs are heavier than fixtures
C] jigs are equal in weight to fixtures for same operation
D] None of these
78] Which fixtures are used for machining parts which musthav-e machined details evenw spaced?
A] Profile fixtures
B] Duplex fixtures
C] Indexing fixtures
D] None of these
79] Chip breaker in a tool is given
A] 'It break the chips into small pieces
B] to have continuous type of chips from long cut
C] to have crushed chips]
80] Step type chip breaker is the one
A] in which a small groove is ground behind the cutting edge
B] in which a step IS ground on the face of the tool along the cutting edge
C] in which a thin carbide plate or clamp is brazed or screwed on the face of the tool]
81] Sine bar is made of
A] high carbon steel
B] high speed steel
C] nickel steel
D] stabilized chromium steel]
82] Sine bar is used for
A] levelling the job for drilling
B] finding the angle of taper job
C] measuring diameter of holes
D] checking profile of thread]
83] Length of sine bar is the distance between
A] one end to another end of sine bar
B] diagonal cross length of the sine bar

C] centre to centre between rollers

D] outside to outside between rollers]

Sine bar Animation & Video

84] The size of a sine bar is specified by it's

A] weight

B] measurement of width

C] length

D] maximum angle of setting]

85]The purpose of providing a stopper at one end of the sine bar is for

A] easy handling

B] preventing the job from slipping]

C] supporting the slip gauge

D] using as a reference while setting]

86] A sine bar is made with four or five equally'spaced holes on its body]
The purpose of these holes is to

A] Handle the sine bar easily

B] Reduce the weight of sin bar

C] Prevent distortion of the top surface of sine bar

D] Give good appearance to the sine bar

87] A sine bar is used for

A] Measuring the diameter of holes '

B] Finding the angle of a taper job

C] Leveling the job for drilling

D] Chuckin'g the profile of a thread

88] For measuring angles using the sine bar the angle framed according
to the ratio between the height of slip gauge and the

A] Height of sine bar

B] Number slip gauge

C] Length of sine bar

D] Width of sine bar

89] -----------is used for checking angle within an accuracy of 1]

A] Gauge

B] Sine bar

C] Temple

D] Telescopic gauge

90] Centre line of the contact rollers and datum surface if the sine bar
are

A] Same line' '

B] Parallel

C] Inclined

D] Perpendicular

91] The sine bar is made of -.

A] High carbon steel

B] Stabilized chromium steel '

C] High speed steel

D] Nicked steel

92] A sine bar with a length of l=200mm is used to check accurately the angle of a Work piece] The angle to be checked: 250 calculate the height 'h' of the slip gauges?

A] 84.54mm

B] 83.52mm

C] 81.81mm

D] 85.52mm

93] Which of the following statement is correct?'

A] Gauges are used to check the size

B] Template are used to chuck-the size

C] Gauges are used to measure the size

D] Gauges are used to check shape of component

94] At what standard temperature are the gauges kept in the section?

A] 100 C

B] 20° C

C] 100 F

D] 20° F

95] Which grade of slip gauge is generally used in workshop?

A] Grade 0

B] Grade l

C] Grade H

D] Grade 0

Slip guage Animation & Video

96] As per Indian Standards a special set gauge is used consisting of

A] 81 Pieces

B] 112 Pieces

C] 120 Pieces

D] 130 Pieces

97] The accuracy of reference gauge is

A] 0.05 mm

B] 0.01 mm

C] 0.001]

D] 0.0001 mm

98] ln case of ant burr on slip gauge, it should be removed by

A] Filling

B] Lapping

C] Scraping

D] Grinding

99] Hardness of slip gauge should be?

A] More than 63 HRC

B] 58 HRC

C] 55 HRC

D] 50 HRC

100]------------- Slip gauge is used for Checking component within an accuracy of 0.01 mm]

A] Workshop gauge

B] Inspection gauge

C] Reference gauge

D] Ring gauge

101], ------------is used for checking accuracy of precision instrument]

A] Gauge block

B] Fader gauge

C] Sine bar

D] Plug gauge

102] Slip gauge are Cleaned before using to ensure accuracy] What medium will you use for this purpose.

A] Oil

B] Thinner

C] Carbon tetrachloride/ White petrol

D] Turpentine oil

103]To check the dimensional accuracy of identical components, a dial test indicator is set-for t 6 Size and used as a comparator] What will you use to set to the dial test indicator?

A] Dial test indicator

B] Teeter gauge

C] Slip gauge

D], surface gauge

104] which one of the following statement about Sine bar is not correct?

A] Uses tow precision rollers kept on either side
B] Made of the Chromium steel
C] The surface is lapped
<u>D] The centrelines of the holes will be inclined to the top surface</u>
105] A slip gauge is a ----------
<u>A] Rectangular block</u>
B] Square block
C] Cubic block
D] Cylindrical block
106] In 4th SERIES of slip gauge, which one of the following range is correct in set 46 pieces
<u>A] 1.0 to 9.0 mm.</u>
B] 1.001 101.009 mm
C] 1.01 to 1.09 mm
D]'1.1'to_-1.9mm
107] In 5th SERIES of slip gauge, which one Of the following range is correct in set 46 pieces –
<u>A] 100to 100 mm '</u>
B] 1.001 to 1.009 mm
C] 1.01 to 0.09mrn
D] 11 to 9mm
108] In 2NDS SERIES of slip gauge, which one of the following range IS correct in set of 45 pieces-
A] 1.0 to 9.0 mm
B] 1.001 to 1] 009 mm
<u>C] 1.01 to 1.09 mm</u>
D] 1.1 to 1.9mm
109] In 3RD SERIES of slip gauge, which one of the following range is correct in set 46 pieces –
A] 10.0 to 100 mm
B] 1.001 to 1.009 mm
C] 1.01 to 1.09 mm
<u>D] 1.1 to 1.9 mm</u>
110] In 1ST SERIES of slip gauge, which one of the following range is correct in set 46 pieces –
<u>A] 0.001mm</u>
B] 001mm
C] 0.1mm

D] 1.0mm

111] In 2ned SERIES of slip gauge, which one of the following STEP is correct in set of 46 pieces –

A] 0.001mm

B] 0.01 mm

C] 0.1 mm

D] 1-0 mm

112] In 3rd SERIES of slip gauge, which one of the following STEP Is correct in set 46 pieces

A] 0.001mm

B] 0.01mm

C] 0.1 mm

D] 1.0mm

113] In following which type of tip for cemented carbide threading tool?

A] For clamping on reject tool

B] with brazing on tool

C] With welding on tool

D] With soldering on tool

114] The tip of a cemented carbide threading tool is

A] brazed

B] welded

C] soldered

D] clamped to the shank

115] Soft soldering is done

A] below 450∘ C

B] above 450∘C

C] at 900∘C

D] above 1000∘C

116] Brazing is done

A] at 1900∘C

B] above 450∘C

C] at 1000∘C

D] below 450∘C

117] A brazed joint is

A] weaker than a soldered joint

B] stronger than a solder join

C] stronger than a welded joint

D] <u>weaker than a silver soldered joint</u>

118] in grinding, the surface speed (cutting speed] is expressed in

A] mm/minute

B] mm/second

C] m/minute

D] <u>m/second</u>

119] The cutting speed for aluminium with H.S.S] tools is

A] 30 m/min

B] 50 m/min

C] 70 m/min

D] <u>130 m/min</u>

120] The cutting speed for brass with a H.S.S] tool is

A] 10 m/min

B] 25 m/min

C] <u>70 m/min</u>

D] 140 m/min

121] The distance, which the cutting edge of a tool passes over the material in a minute while machining is Know as...

A] RPM

B] Feed

C] Machine speed

D] <u>Cutting speed</u>

122] The depth of cut for M24 x 3 mm internal thread is

A] <u>0.5412 x 3</u>

B] 0.6134 x 3

C] 0.5 x 3

D] 0.7 x 3

123] To cut 24 x 3 mm internal acme threads, the core diameter of the job is

A] 20.00 mm

B] 21.66 mm

C] 21.00 mm

D] <u>20.60 mm</u>

124] The depth of cut for metric square threading is

A] 0.6 x P

B] <u>0.5 x P</u>

C] 0.5412 x P

D] 0.6412 x P

Thread Animation & Video

125] To cut buttress thread, the depth of cut is

A] 0.5412 x P

B] 0.6 x P

C] 0.7 x P

D] 0.75 x P

126] Lubricant is necessary to ....]

A] run the machine smoothly taking least load

B] Run the machine quickly

C] Stop the machine immediately

D] Produce work piece of greater accuracy

127] Extreme pressure additive (EPA] is mixed with cutting fluid for improving its power of.

A] Cooling

B] Lubrication

D] Production of the machined surface

C] Cleaning of cutting zone

128] The main purpose for using a lubricant in machine tools is to ------

A] Cool down the making parts

B] Prevent machine tool from heating

C] Wet the making parts for close contact

D] Minimize the friction between the making parts

129] Preventive maintenance is ....]

A] The maintenance involves the use of sensitive instruments

B] The maintenance generally performed by operator himself

C] The work carried only when machine break down

D] plan to minimize the unforeseen break down

130] What is a break down maintenance?

A] Maintenance to minimize the unforeseen breakdown

B] Maintenance generally performed by operator himself

C] Maintenance involves replacement of worn out parts

D] Repairs work carried only when machine breakdown

131] The Routine Maintenance is ---------

A] it is planned maintenance to minimize the unforeseen breakdown

B] This type of maintenance involves the use of sensitive instrument

C] It is repair work carried only when machine breakdowns

D] This types of maintenance is generally performed by operator himself

132] The reference surface during marking is provided by the...

A] Surface gauge

B] Workpiece

C] Drawing of the work

D] <u>Marking table surface</u>

133] The reference surface during marking is provided by the...

A] Surface gauge

B] Workpiece

C] Drawing of the work

D] <u>Marking table surface</u>

134] Surface plates are made of...

A] High grade cast steel

B] <u>Fine-grained cast iron</u>

C] Alloy steels

D] Wrought iron

135] Ribs are given on the unmachined portion of the angle plate for...

A] Easy handling

B] Convenience in manufacturing

C] Clamping while setting on machines

D] <u>Rigidity and to prevent distortion</u>

136] The slots on the angle plate are given for...

A] Reducing weight

B] Aligning the work

C] Lifting using hooks

D] <u>Accommodating bolts</u>.

137] The size of the angle plates is stated by...

A] Weight

B] Length

C] Length x width

D] <u>Size number</u>

138] The Gear ratio required for cutting a screw thread of 2.5 mm on a lathe having a lead screw pitch using single point cutting tool is ----

A] <u>1:2</u>

B] 2:1

C] 1:1 mm

139] Threading tools are checked for accuracy for the 60° angle by using a

A] Thread plug gauge

B] <u>centre gauge</u>

C] screw pitch gauge

D] tool angle gauge

140] The number of threads per inch can be checked with a

A] tool gauge

B] metric rule by counting

C] ring gauge

D] screw pitch gauge

screw pitch gauge Animation & Video

141] Which gauge is used to check the threading tool of lathe, for accuracy on the 60° angle?

A] Screw pitch gauge

B] Thread plug gauge

C] Centre gauge

D] Thread ring gauge

142] Tool maker's buttons are used to

A] adjust the slackness in the guide ways oi crossslide

B] alter the tool height

C] align the work for boring to a given datum

D] none of the above]

143] The space clearance between bore and screw is provided

A] for shifting the button position

B] for easy change of button

C] for lubricating bush

D] for easy clamping of button]

144] Normally button boring operations on irregular shaped heavy jobs are carried out in

A] three jaw chuck(universal]

B] faceplate

C] betwccn centres

D] four jaw independent chuck]

145] Tool maker's buttons are made ot]

A] plastic

B] cast iron

C] hardened steel

D] bronze]

146] The smallest inside micrometer has the graduation marked on the sleeve

A] 10mm

B] 12mm

C] 13mm

D] 25mm

Inside micrometer Animation & Video

147] The method used to out multiple start thread is

A] forward and reverse switch method

B] use half nut method]

C] face plate and indexing drive plate method

D] attachment method]

148] Multiple start threads are used on

A] vice spindle

B] lathe Spindle

C] standard nut

D] pen cover]

149] Balancing is done in the face plate work

A] to increase the speed

B] to reduce the pressure on the tool

C] for uniform rotation of work

D] to get a good finish

150] A face plate is used to hold

A] a round job

B] a finished job

C] an irregular Job

D] a hollow job

151] Surface plates are made of...

A] High grade cast steel

B] Fine-grained cast iron

C] Alloy steels

D] Wrought iron

152] An irregular shaped work piece is turned on a Lathe] Which one of the following work holding accessories is used?

A] Two Jaw chuck

B] Three Jaw chuck

C] Driving plate

D] Face plate

153] Ribs are given on the unmachined portion of the angle plate for...

A] Easy handling

B] Convenience in manufacturing

C] Clamping while setting on machines

D] <u>Rigidity and to prevent distortion</u>

154] The slots on the angle plate are given for...

A] Reducing weight

B] Aligning the work

C] Lifting using hooks

D] <u>Accommodating bolts</u>.

155] The size of the angle plates is stated by...

A] Weight

B] Length

C] Length x width

D] <u>Size number</u>

156] Which is correct angle plate used with face plate

(A] <u>Solid Type</u>

(B] Box Type

(C] Adjustable Type

(D] None of them

157] Face plate is made from.....]

(A] Mild Steel

(B] <u>Cast Iron</u>

(C] Brass

(D] Aluminium

158] When angle plate is used on Lathe Machine some weight~ clamping on another side is called.....

(A] Catch Plate

(B] Back Plate

(C] Face Plate

(D] <u>Angle Plate</u>

159] To clamp the work piece against the face of an angle plate----------------are used]

A] Chuck

B] <u>C clamps</u>

C] Spindle

D] Vice

160] The Slot are provided on angle plate for ---------------

A] <u>Accommodating bolts</u>

B] Hanging with hooks

C] Reducing weight

D] Aligning the work

161] The included angle of the groove of 'V' block is always....

A] 45°

B] 60°

C] 90°

D] <u>120°</u>

162] 'V' blocks are available in grades of...

A] <u>A & B</u>

B] A,B & C

C] 1,2 & 3

D] 1 & 2

163] 'V' blocks of grade 'B' are made of

A] <u>Cast iron</u>

B] Mild steel

C] Steel

D] Cast steel

164] Surface plates are made of...

A] High grade cast steel

B] <u>Fine-grained cast iron</u>

C] Alloy steels

D] Wrought iron

165] Clamps are used for the purpose of...

A] Carrying materials from machine to machine

B] <u>Preventing movement of work</u>

C] Preventing scratch on machined components

D] Maintaining accurancy

166] The jig bush used for drilling and reaming of a hole is...?

A] Press fit bush

B] Liner bush

C] <u>Slip renewable bush</u>

D] Fixed renewable bush

167]The portion of the shaft, which is carried in the bearing is called ....

(A] <u>Bearing Body</u>

(B] Inner Race

(C] 0uter Race

(D] Cage

168] In case of plain bearing to prevent the rotation of bush, the bearing it should be fitted with..........]

(A] Welding

(B] O ring

(C] Brazing

(D] Screw or key

169] In which one bearing from the following the loading is parallel to bearing axis?

(A] Solid bearing

(B] Thrust bearing

(C] Roller bearing

(D] self aligning bush bearing

170]This bearings from the following are] Made in two halves and assembled in special Plummer blocks?

(A] Solid bearing

(B] Bearing

(C] Spit bearing

(D] Adjustable lid bearing

171]Which among the following type of bearing has a spherical bore on its race?

(A] Angular contact ball bearing

(B] Self aligning ball bearing

(C] Roller bearing

(D] Thrush ball bearing

172]What is the reason of reducing friction in roller bearing?

(A] Contact area

(B] Grease

(C] sites

173]It is necessary to have the Outside diameter of the bearing severally restricted due to limited bearing space in housing Select the bearing.

(A] Ball bearing

(B] Roller bearing

(C] Needle bearing

(D] Any of the above

174] Name of the bearing which have barrel shaped rollers and spherical bores in the outer race?

(A] Self aligning roller bearings

(B] Roller bearing

(C] Roller bearing

(D] Needle bearing

175]The material of races and rolling elements of anti-fliction bearing ....]

(A] Chromium steel or Chrome-nickel steel]

(B] Stainless steel]

(C] Cast iron]

(D] Bronze

176]When the anti-friction bearing is mounted right into the shaft] Pressure should be applied on this part.......]

(A] Inner race

(B] Outer race

(C] Cage

(D] Rolling elements

177]The heating temperature of bearing in -oil bath or induction heating process]

(A] (50°C to 90°C

(B] 90°C to 100°C

(C] 90°C to 120°C

(D] 90°C to 150°C

178] Rolling contact bearing should not be heated more than temperature]

A] 100°C

B] 120°C

C] 140°C

D] 150°C

179] Which among the following bearing material has a low load carting capacity?

(A] Cadmium based alloy

(B] White metal

(C] Lead bronze

(D] Cast iron

180]Identify the name of bearing metal which are tin based or lead based?

A] Lead bronze

B] Copper lead alloy

C] White metal

D] Brass

181]Bush bearing is made from.....]

(A] Gun metal / Bronze

(B] Cast iron

(C] Aluminium alloy

(D] None of the above

182]According to general rule the temperature of bearing should not be more than .....] temperature.

(A] 60°C to 70°C]

(B] 150°C to 160°C

(C] 200°C to 210°C

(D] 250°C to 260°C

183]Which among the following bearing metal's bearings works at higher temperature and carry the higher loads?

(A] anagram

(B] Cadmium based alloy

(C] Aluminium alloys

(D] Lead bronze

184]The purpose of making bearing metals by sintering process is...

(A] Providing porosity in the metal

(B] Making solid structure

(C] Increasing the strength of metal

(D] None of the above

185]Which among the following material's bearings are used in situations where lubrication is difficult?

(A] Cadmium based alloy

(B] Lead alloys

(C] Mustered alloys

(D] Aluminium alloys

186]Which among the following material's bearings need not lubrication?

(A] Cast iron]

(B] Melon

(C] White metal

(D] Aluminium alloys

187]Which among the following bearing material is best for hard journals?

(A] Cast iron

(B] melon

(C] Lead bronze

(D] Aluminium alloys

188] The following given which device is used for holding job & guide for toll while working?

A] Gauge

B] Housing

C] Jig

D] Fixture

Fixture Animation & Video

189] The following given device which one for used clamping job only?

A] Jig

B] Fixture

C] Housing

D] Gauge

190] While fabricated by welding job which device is used for holding fixed or revolving if necessary up to 360°C of welding job?

A] Gauge

b] Template

C] Jig

D] Fixture

191] The main things of drilling jig its not clamping with machine table which reason is correct given following?

A] it is strong for operation

B] it is easy for operation

C] many different size holes produce by different setting while drilling on job

D] for this device has lot of time

192] Following which locations is most usefull for round shape job location?

A] pin type locator

B] wedge type locator

C] vee locator

D] adjustable stop locators

193] Following which reason is scorrect for using bushing in drilling jigs?

A] easy for drilling

B] for fixed drill hole size

C] for accurate drilling operation

D] for given better finish drilling hole

Jig Animation & Video

194] The metal for manufacturing jig bush is...?

A] mild steel

B] cast iron

C] cast steel

D] tool steel

195] Given following bush which busing used for locating renewable bushing?

A] press fit bushing

B] linear bushing

C] special bushing

D] knurd bushing

196] jig has tolerance..?

A] five present of job tolerance

B] ten percent of job tolerance

C] 20% to 50% of job tolerance

D] 100% of job tolerance

197] Following which jig is use for location from bore?

A] plate jig

B] solid jig

C] post jig

D] box jig

198] Following which jig having drill plate?

A] solid jig

B] plate jig

C] box jig

D] table jig

199] Fixture is used for.......

(A] Job Truing

(B] For guided cutting

(C] For clamping

200] Angle fixture is made at.......] °

(A] 90°

(B] 120°

(C] 45°

(D] 60°

201]The fixture it is uSe for Lathe Operation is called

(A] Milling Fixture

(B] Turning Fixture

(C] Drilling Fixture

(D] Shaping Fixture

202] Heating plain carbon steel uniformly above the lower critical temperature, casuses the commencement Of the formation of solid solution called...

A] Ferrite

B] Pearlite

C] Austenite

D] Martensite

203] The process of heating and cooling for changing the structure of steel for obtaining the required properties is called...

A] Hardening

B] Heat treatment

C] Normalising

D] Tempering

204] The main purposes of annealing is

A] To increase the hardness

B] To increase the toughness

C] To improve machinability

D] To remove distoration

205] The process which helps in producing a fine grain for uniformity of structure and for improved mechanical properties is known as...

A] Tempering

B] Annealing

C] Hardening

D] Normalising

206] Which one of the following is an alloy of carbon and iron, in which carbon is in a combined state?

A] Steel

B] Wrought iron

C] Cast iron

D] Pig-iron

207] Carbon dissolved in the iron to form a solid solution is called

A] Cementite

B] Ferrite

C] Pearlite

D] Austenite

208] A chemical compound of carbon with iron is called...

A] Ferrite

B] Pearlite

C] <u>Cementite</u>

D] Austenite

209] Cementite and ferrite will together form a laminated structure in the steel which is called...

A] Martensite

B] Alloy steel

C] Austenite

D] <u>Pearlite</u>

210] Increase of carbon content in carbon steel beyond 0.83% results in proportional..

A] Reduction of elasticity

B] <u>Increases in hardness</u>

C] Increase in strength

D] Increase in ductility

211] Which one of the following is thermoplastics?

A] Phenolics

B] Aminos

C] <u>Acrylic resin</u>

D] Polyster resin

212] Which one of the following comes under thermosetting plastics category?

A] Cellulosics

B] Nylon

C] <u>Epoxy</u>

D] Polythene

213]The purpose of normalising steel is ....

(A] <u>Remove induced stresses</u>

(B] Improve machinability

(C] Soften the steel

(D] Increase the toughness and reduce brittleness

214]A carbon steel piece is heated just above 730°C maintained at that temperature for a few hours and then slowly cooled] What heat treatment process is carried out?

(A] Normalizing

(B] Case hardening

(C] Hardening

(D] Annealing

215]The toughness in a steel is increased and brittleness is decreased by a heat treatment operation called as......

A] Annealing

B] Normalizing

C] Tempering

D] Case hardening

216]Cyaniding and nitrating are two methods of.......]

A] Hardening

B] Case hardening

C] Tempering

D] Ammonising

217] The external surface of mild steel parts can be hardened by.....]

A] Tempering

B] Normalising

C] Hardening

D] Hardening

218]In nitrating process the NH_3, gas is introduced at ....

A] 500°C 2 560°C

B] 600°C 3 650°C

C] 575°C 3 600°C

D] 650°C 3 700°

219]High speed steel is tempered at ......]

A] 220°C 3 230°C

B] 280°C '6 400°C

C] 230°C '3 270°C

D] 550°C 3 600°C

220]Which one of the following process is used for surface hardening the of tool steel?

A] Carburising

B] Cyaniding

C] Induction hardening

D] Hardening

221]Lower critical temperature of higher" hon steel while hardening is.......

A] 960°C

B] 900°C

C] 723°C

D] 560°C

222]Approximate hardness of H.S.S] milling cutters is.........

A] 45HRCA

B] 52 HRC

C] 62 HRC

D] 75 HRC

223]What is the main purpose of annealing]

A] To improve machinability

B] To improve magnetism

C] To increase hardness

D] To increase toughness

224]Which one of the following is the solid early uprising material?

A] Charcoal

B] Petrol

C] Ammonia

D] Kerosene

225]While hardening after heating the steel to the required temperature it is held at that temperature as soaking time for normally]

A] 5 minutes for 10 mm thickness

B] 10 minutes for 5 mm thickness

C] 20 minutes for 2 mm thickness

D] 20 minutes for 2 mm thickness

226]Which one of the following quenching medium is used for hardening H.S.S] tool?

A] Water

B] Brine solution

C] Oil

D] Soda Water

227]The hardening temperature for high speed steel tool is......

A] 1250°C

B] 950°C

C] 850°C

D] 750°C

228]Which one of the following is the purpose of tempering a hardened steel.

A] To increase to toughness

B] To increase ductility

C] To increase hardness

D] To reduce hardness

229]While normalising the steel should be cooled....

A] In still air to room temperature

B] In oil

C] In forced air

D] In water

230]The process of increasing carbon percentage on the surface of low carbon steel is known as......

A] Hardening

B] Manning

C] Carburising

D] Tempering

231]The process of producing a component with tough and ductile core and a hard outer surface is known as.....]

A] Hardening

B] Case hardening

C] Tempering

D] Annealing

232]The process of heating steel to about 400C above the upper critical temperature and cooling it in still air to room temperature is known .....

A] Hardening

B] Annealing

C] Normalizing / grain running

D] Tempering

233] Which one of the following heat treatment process produces a scale-free surface on the component?

A] Flame Hardening

B] Case Hardening

C] Normalizing

D] Induction Hardening

234]The point angle of the indenter of vickcr hardness tester is.....]

A] 120°

B] 130°

C] 136°

D] 140°

235]Load range for B scale of Rockwell hardness tester ......

A] 5 kgf to 120 kgf

B] 10 kgf to 100 kgf

C] 10 kgf to 150 kgf

D] 100 kgf to 3000 kgf

236] The major load applied for Rockwell hardness testing method in '3' scale is 3....

A] 300 kgf

B] 15 kgf

C] 120 kgf

D] 100 kgf

237] The difference in reading between the minor and major load is taken into account' in......]

A] Brinell lmrdnless Test

B] Rockwell Hardness Test

C] Shore hardness Test

D] Vickers hardness Test

238] The process of heating and cooling to change the structure of steel for obtaining the required properties is called

A] Hardening

B] Normalizing

C] Heat treatment

D] Tempering

239] The main purpose of annealing is to

A] Increase the hardness

B] Increase the toughness

C] Improve machinability

D] Improve distortion

240] The purpose of normalizing steel is to -----------

A] Remove the induced Stress

B] Improve genes and reduce brittleness

C] Soften the metal

D] Increase the surface?

241] Which one of the following process is used for hardenmg the outer 5" Annealing

A] Hardening

B] Tempering

C] Case Hardening

D] Tear surface

242] The purpose of producmg a component with tough and ductIIe core and hard ou is known as.....]

A] Hardening

B] Case hardening

C] Tempering

D] annealing

243] Lower critical temperature of high carbon steel while hardening is ----------

A] 9600C

B] 900°C

c] 7230 c

D] 56O C

244] The process of Changing the structure and thus changing the properties by heating and 'cooling is known as --

A] Heat treatment

B] Alloying

C] Tempering

D] None of these

245] For refining the grain structure which one of the following heat treatment processes 'Is adopted]

A] Annealing

B] Hardening

C] Tempering

D] Normalising

246] Annealing is performed on iron and steel ---------

A] To remove internal stresses

B] To reduce hardness

C] To improve machinability

D] All of these

247] Which one of the following does not fall under the stages of heat treatment?

A] Heating

B] Cleaning

C] Quenching

D] Soaking

CNC Machine Tape Punch

image

248] Tape punch having 1 inch in width tape it is made by

A] Paper Mylar

B] Aluminum Mylar

C] Plastic

D] Above all

249] In point two point positioning positioning system........] Is acceptable

A] Open loop control system

B] Closed loop control system

C] Above both

D] None of them

250] In CNC machine having.......

A] Lead screw

B] Ball lead screw

C] Above both

D] None of both

CNC Program Coordinate

251] The aim of sub program is........

A] For find coordinates X Y Z.

B] For other small machine.

C] To avoid cutting tool nose tool nose penetration in Jobs surface of high speed.

D] While machining of job in special condition do not use time to time of program block.

252] What is mean by while while xyz co-ordinate point measure zero-measurement

A] Reference mark.

B] Work zero

C] Co-ordinate points

<u>D] Above all</u>

253] CNC machine specified by axis......

A] 2 axis

B] 3 axis

C] 4 axis

<u>D] Above all</u>

<u>CNC Machine Axis</u>

image

254] Xyz axis of CNC machines which point is used for measurements.

<u>A] Work zero point</u>

B] Machine zero point

C] Common zero point

D] Above all

255] Following which point is not useful in CNC machine.

A] various operation done on CNC machine.

B] Less amount for inspection.

C] Hard for setting measure.

<u>D] Machine efficiency is depend upon operators skill.</u>

256] For selection of zero offset before necessary..........

A] cutter is fixed on machine table.

B] The data entered in machine.

C] Job is fixed on machine table.

<u>D] Speed and feed selection necessary before machine operates.</u>

<u>CNC Work Zero Offset Setting.</u>

257] In zero offset program indicates........] Code of following

A] X y z

<u>B] X0 y0 z00</u>

C] X10 Y20 Z30

D] G71

258] Work zero is

A] Datum of machine zero on job position.

B] Indicate by X0Y0Z0.

C] Selection of point on job according to program.

D] The end of machining point

259] M command is used for starting operation and complete revolution cycle M03 means.

A] Stop the program.

B] Program completed and reset.

C] Complete the program.

D] Spindle clockwise motion.

CNC Machine Lubrication

image

260] CNC machine is not manually operated it is control by...........

A] Program

B] operation

C] Cam

D] Plug board system

261] In CNC machine M13 means

A] coolant stop

B] coolant on

C] spindle stop

D] coolant on & spindle on

262] The function of power pack in CNC machine.

A] For balancing of lubricants heat.

B] For increasing heat of lubricants.

C] For destroy heat of lubricant.

D] Above all.

CNC Machine Bed.

263] The section of CNC machine bed is.....

A] Flat

B] Half round

C] Rectangular

D] Triangular

264] Following which statement is disadvantage of CNC machine.

A] Less inspection charge.

B] Less tooling charge.

C] Increase production rate.

D] High establishment charge.

265] The point to point system is more effective for......

A] Turning

B] Profile milling

C] Grinding

D] Drilling

Tool Setting on NC Machine.

266] Tool setting on NC machine on......] unit.

A] Presetting device.

B] Order special device without machine.

C] On n c machine other empty time.

D] When other operation working on machine.

267] For measuring system having built-in coordinates in this system..........] is called zero position.

A] Reference point.

B] Machine zero point.

C] Work zero point

D] Program zero point.

268] Job turning on CNC machine 50 mm dia turn with programs said the trial run 50.1 mm at production time following which Idea used for correct dia making

A] by increase offset of tool 0.1 mm.

B] by increase offset of tool 0.05 mm

C] by decrease offset of tool 0.05 mm

D] by decrease offset of tool 0.1 mm

CNC Copying Lathe Machine.

269] For measure zero offset dim dimensions on CNC machine.........mode is set

A] MDI

B] Jog

C] Automatic

D] preset

270] Coping unit of copying lathe is work on

A] Mechanical power system

B] Hand power system

C] Hydraulic power system

D] None of them

271] Following which advantage of Pneumatic power system

A] For increase production rate.

B] Less cash for layout

C] Good climate for work

D] Above all

Principle of CNC Machine Templates.

272] For face copying........] Type template is used

A] Rounded

B] Plate type

C] Flat

D] Triangular

273].............] Is Main principle of CNC MACHINE?

A] Indicate all states in numbers

B] More time required for mechanical control on machine.

C] Cutting speed is more than manual control.

D] Production sequence in workshop is stored by block number in machine.

274] For copy of one shaft.......] Type template is used.

A] Rounded

B] Triangular

C] Flats

D] Square

CNC Program Tool Path.

275] The symptoms of continuous path is

A] Called counting system.

B] Tool and work piece on co-ordinate Axis for inter related motion.

C] By the setting of cutter feed and speed

D] Above all

276] Misc command M30 means........

A] End of program and reset

B] Program stop

C] Clockwise motion of spindle

D] Complete the programs

277] Following which affect on milling surface while by milling with unsetting spindle vertical milling machine with- longitudinal feed.

A] Convex surface

B] Concave surface

C] Radius cross line

D] Rough surface

CNC Milling Operation]

278] While milling by vertical milling machine with 12 mm dia end mill cutter through slot provide on mild steel plate the cutter is sleep and broken for this fault how it is avoid.

A] High speed spindle

B] Low cutting speed

C] Increase of cut depth

D] Less the depth and feed of cutter

279] Having 5 mm pitch of screw and dividing ratio of 40 : 1 what is lead of milling machine

A] 0.25 mm

B] 5 mm

C] 8 mm

D] 200 mm

280] If not use of backlash Eliminator slap cutter used for down milling operation which safety to be observed?

A] Less lead and depth

B] High lead

C] high lead and less depth

D] High lead and high speed

CNC Machine Zero & Feed Rate.

281] Zero offset is the distance between.....] And.........

A] G41 & g42

B] Machine zero & work zero

C] Reference point and tapping mode

D] None of them

282] The feed rate is programmed as mm per minute with G ....] And mm per- Revolution with G.

A] G41 & g42

B] G 43 and G 40

C] G 94 and g95

D] None of them

283] For collection all instructions from.......] In CNC control unit

A] Memory

B] Tape reader

C] Control panel

D] Operator

CNC Drilling Machine.

cnc   drilling

machine.jpg

284] For control forward and backward of- CNC drilling machine y axis.........

A] Spindle

B] Table

C] Clockwise

D] Column

285] M 01 command means.....

A] For stopping programs

B] End of program and reset

C] Stopping programs condition

D] Clockwise rotation of machine spindle

286] CNC machine is founded by American scientist john person in.......] Year

A] 1950

B] 1952

C] 1955

D] 1957

CNC Control, Input & Memory Unit.

287] Name of unit used to command the CNC machine.

A] Control unit

B] Memory unit
C] Input unit
D] Output unit
288] Name of unit used to processing the data in CNC machine.
A] Memory unit
B] Control unit
C] Input unit
D] Output unit
289] Name of unit used to storing the data in CNC machine.
A] Input unit
B] Control unit
C] Memory unit
D] Output unit
Servo Motor in CNC Machine.
servo motor.jpg   290] Name of unit used to calculation of

data in CNC machine.
A] Output unit
B] Arithmetic unit
C] Memory unit
D] Input unit
291] Name of unit used to display result of processing data in CNC machine
A] Arithmetic unit
B] Output unit
C] Memory unit
D] Input unit
292] Servo Motor in CNC machine is used to..............
A] Changing tool on machine spindle
B] Driving machine spindle
C] Fixing job on machine spindle
D] Proving job on spindle

<u>Types of CNC Machine.</u>

293] One of the below part of CNC machine used to changing tools on spindle.

A] Servo Motor

B] Control panel

<u>C] Automatic tool changer A T C</u>

D] High speed spindle

294] One of the below CNC machine in CNC milling category is.......

A] Chucking centre

B] CNC late

<u>C] Vertical machining centre</u>

D] Surface grinding machine

295] One of the below CNC machine in turning centre or CNC lathe category is.......

A] Vertical machining centre

B] Horizontal machining centre

<u>C] Vertical turning centre</u>

D] Profile grinding machine

<u>Miscellaneous Functions for CNC Machine.</u>

296] One of the below CNC machine in grinding Centre category is.....

A] Universal milling centre

<u>B] Cylindrical grinding machine</u>

C] CNC late

D] Vertical machining centre

Grinding Wheel Animation & Video

297] In CNC Machine programming word M indicates

A] Feed rate

B] Spindle speed

<u>C] Miscellaneous function</u>

D] Tool number

298] In CNC Machine programming preparatory function G00 is for.....

<u>A] Linear interpolation</u>

B] Clockwise circular interpolation

C] Counter clockwise circular interpellation

D] Hold

<u>Preparatory Functions for CNC Machine.</u>

299] In CNC Machine programming preparatory function G02 is for.....

A] Linear interpolation

B] Clockwise circular interpolation

C] Counter clockwise circular interpellation

D] Hold

300] One of the bellow preparatory function G 00 is used in CNC program for.........

A] Linear interpellation or feed motion in straight line.

B] Clockwise circular interpellation

C] Point to point Positioning or Rapid motion.

D] Counter clockwise circular interpellation

301] One of the bellow preparatory function used in CNC program for 3D interpellation

A] G 05

B] G12

C] G17

D] G18

Threading & Tapping on CNC Machine.

302] One of the bellow preparatory you function used in CNC program for thread cutting constant lead

A] G33

B] G40

C] G53

D] G62

303] One of the bellow preparatory function used in CNC program for tapping operation.

A] G-40

B] G53

C] G62

D] G63

304] One of the below preparatory function used in CNC program for milling operation.

A] G62

B] G63

C] G 78, 79

D] G81

Drilling, Boring & Reaming on CNC Machine

305] One of the bellow preparatory function used in CNC program for drilling operation.

A] G 81

B] G 82

C] G 84

D] G 85

306] One of the bellow preparatory function used in CNC program for reaming operation.

A] G 84

B] G 85

C] G 86

D] G 90

307] One of the below preparatory function used in CNC program for boring operation.

A] G 86

B] G 90

C] G 91

D] G 92

CNC Program Sequence Number.

308] In CNC program which letter is used to indicate the sequence number of the block

A] N

B] G

C] F

D] S

309] In CNC program which letter is used to indicate position of linear axis

A] ABC

B] UVW

C] XYZ

D] IJK

310] One of the below letters used in CNC program for Feed rate

A] S

B] F

C] T

D] M

Tool Change & Spindle Speed in CNC Machine.

tool change i cnc.jpg

ATC Automatic Tool Changer Animation & Video

311] One of the below letters used in CNC program for spindle speed in RPM

A] M

B] T

C] S

D] F

312] In CNC program which letter is used to indicate TOOL function number of tool

A] T

B] S

C] M

D] F

313] In CNC program which miscellaneous function used to program stop

A] M03

B] M00

C] M01

D] M02

CNC Machine Spindle Direction.

314] One of the below miscellaneous function used to program optional Stop

A] M 01

B] M 02

C] M 03

D] M 04

315] In CNC program miscellaneous function M02 is used to......

A] Program stop

B] Optional program stop

C] End of program

D] Clockwise spindle on

316] In CNC program miscellaneous function M03 is used to..........

A] Counter clockwise spindle on

B] Clockwise spindle on

C] Spindle off

D] Tool change

Coolant in CNC Machine.

coolant in cnc machine.jpg

CNC Coolant Pump Animation & Video

317] One of the below miscellaneous function used in CNC program for spindle stop.

A] M04

B] M05

C] M06

D] M07

318] In CNC program which miscellaneous function is used for Tools change

A] M06

B] M07

C] M09

D] M10

319] One of the below miscellaneous function used in CNC program for coolant on

A] M08

B] M09

C] M10

D] M11

Clamping the Job on CNC Machine.

320] One of the below miscellaneous function in CNC program used for coolant off

A] M11

B] M10

C] M9

D] M15

321] In CNC program which miscellaneous function used for clamping the job on machine table.

A] M09

B] M10

C] M11

D] M15

322] One of the below miscellaneous function in CNC program used for unclamp the job

A] M11

B] M15

C] M30

D] M60

Work piece change in CNC Machine.

323] In CNC program which miscellaneous function used for change of workpiece

A] M30

B] M60

C] M68

D] M78

324] The machine is.........for zero off-setting on CNC Machine.

A] In MDI Mode

B] In JOG Mode

C] In Automatic Mode

D] In Present Mode

325] The feed rate on NC Machine is indicate by ......code.

A] X

B] Y

C] F

D] Z

CNC Machine Axis Position]

326] The position of axis is indicate by.......code.

A] X,Y,Z

B] P,Q,R

C] A,B,C

D] M,N,O

327] CNC Drilling Machine is on.......Axis Programmed.

A] Two Axis

B] Three Axis

C] Four Axis

D] Six Axis

328] From.......unit collect instruction in control unit of CNC

A] Machine Tool

B] Instruction

C] Magnetic Box

D] Memory

Working Graph of CNC Machine]

329] For preparing tape of NC Machine----------code is used.

A] EIA Code

B] ISO Code

C] ASC Code

D] None of them.

330] CNC Machine gives more accurate production than convention machine, But it is more expensive because.

A] It has AC cabin

B] It has dust proof cabin

C] It has strong foundation

D] It has more space

331] CNC Machine is working on graphical base the point on digital line, indicated digital points call..........

A] Graph

B] Input Media

C] Co-Ordinate

D] Original Point

Axis Rotary Motion in CNC Machine]

332] On CNC Machine for longitudinal feed has.......axes, cross feed......axis and for vertical feed........axis name given.

A] A,B,C

B] X,Y,Z

C] P,Q,R

D] M,N,O

333] For rotary motion CNC machine axis has.......name given.

A] A,B,C

B] X,Y,Z

C] P,Q,R

D] M,N,O

334] CNC Machine means.......

A] Natural Control Machine

B] Pneumatic control Machine

C] Numerical Control Machine

D] No Command Machine

335] The size of parts made by .....] for provide interchange ability properties]

(A] Measurement System

(B] Trial and Error System

(C] Limit and Tolerance System

(D] None of Them

Limit fit tolerance Animation & Video

336] In Mass Production for Quality Control the Production is Manufacture......

(A] Zero Defects

(B] Try Method]

(C] Trial and Error

(D] In Limit Size

337] Interchange ability is using for.....]

(A] For Maintenance

(B] For Mass Production

(C] For Single Piece Manufacturing

(D] For Trial and Error Method

338] Which one of the following is important factor required to achieve the interchange ability in mass production?]

A] Geometrical accuracy]

B] Standardization

C] Dimensional accuracy

D] Surface finish

339] Interchange ability is normally applied for? _

A] Repairing of parts

B] Mass production

C] Single piece production

D] All of these

340] inspection aims at

A segregation of defective components

B conformance of rejection

C prevention of rejection

D sale quality goods]

341] Who is responsible for quality?

A designer

B inspector

C operator

D ail]

342] A failure cost reporting system is used for

A incentive for operators

B inventory control

C finding weak points in design

D finding weak spots in production]

343] The stops and trips are used to

A minimise delays for measuring and gauging

B minimise delays in setting tools

C reduce the number of tools needed

D reduce the time required to set work]

344] The term surface finish refers to the...

A] Shining of a machined surface

B] Type of coating given on a surface

C] Heat treatment given on a surface

D] Roughness or smoothness of a surface

345] The purpose for which lapping operation are carried out ---

A] To refine surface finish]

B] To improve quality of fit

C] To improve geometrical accuracy,

D] All the above

346] Which one of the following is a cold working process by which improvement of surface finish, dimensional accuracy and work hardening can be affected without removal of metal?

A] Burnishing

B] Honing

C] Lapping _

D] Super finishing

347] In the honing Process, the movement of the spindle is ---' -----------

A] Vertical and reciprocating

B] Reciprocating

C] Vertical

D] Horizontal and reciprocating

348] lt is the process carried out by using abrasive stick?

A] Lapping B] Honing

C] Super finishing ' D] Burnishing

INDUSTRIAL TRAINING INSTITUTE

Monthly Test-1, Marks- 20, Date:- ________________

(Every Question Carry Two Marks)

1-1] How many types of Lathe as per manufacturing?

A] Two

B] Three

C] Four

D] Five

2-2] How many types of Centre Lathe?

A] Two

B] Three

C] Four

D] Five

3-3] How many types of production lathe?

A] Two

B] Three

C] Four

D] Five

4-4] Which type of lathe is Roller Lathe?

A] Bench Lathe

B] Special Lathe

C] Production Lathe

D] Centre Lathe

5-5] For mass-production which machine is used?

A] Centre Lathe

B] Production Lathe

C] Special Lathe

D] Engine Lathe

6-6] Which lathe is used for more accurate job?

A] Centre Lathe

B] Special Lathe

C] Production Lathe

D] Tool Room Lathe

7-7] The accuracy of Tool Room Lathe is...] to Compeer Centre Lathe.]

(A] Less

(B] More

(C] Very Less

(D] Equal

8-8] In Locomotive Assemble Wheel with Axel is turning on ......Lathe

(A] Centre Lathe

(B] Tool Room Lathe

(C] Wheel Lathe

(D] Gap Bed Lathe

9-9] Cast iron is used for manufacturing machine beds because -------

A] it can resist more compressive stress

B] it is heavy in weight

C] It is cheaper metal

D] It is a brittle metal

10-10] Which one of the following operations can't be performed on a Center Lathe?]

A] Turning

B] Thread cutting

C] Gear cutting

D] Taper turning

INDUSTRIAL TRAINING INSTITUTE

Monthly Test-2, Marks- 20, Date:- _______________

(Every Question Carry Two Marks)

1-20] Form turning done for this purpose....?

A] For attractive job

B] for large material cutting

C] for better finishing

D] for smallest cut on job

2-21] Which type of metal tool use for mass production of form turning?

A] H.S.S]

B] H.C.S]

C] Carbide

D] Cementite

3-22] What is template?

A] One of the cutting operation

B] One of the form turning

C] same figure of the job

D] one of the tool

4-23] Which purpose use template?

A] For marking & checking

B] for threading

C] for turning

D] for measuring

5-24] Which material is use for making template?

A] H.C.S] plate

B] Special tool steel

C] brass or copper

d] G.I] sheet or M.S] thin sheet

6-25] ---------------is used for checking shape of component

A] Template

B] Snap gauge

C] Instrument

D] Sine bar

7-26] The dial test indicator shows the measurement as.....

A] the actual size of the component

B] the difference between the two steps of 5 mm

C] the magnified small variations in sizes throut a pointer

D] the direct reading of the dimension

8-27] The principle of working of the dial test indicator is

A the linear motion is converted into reciprocating motion using slotted link

B the linear motion is converted into rotary motion using rack and pinion

C magnifications of small variation using lenses

D magnifications by electronic means:

9-28] Which of the following instrument is used to check the concentricity of the outside diameter...?

A] Outside micrometer

B] Dial test indicator

C] Vernier caliper

D] Dial calliper

10-29] Which one of the following mechanism is used to convert the linear motion of the plunger of a dial test indicator to the rotary motion of the pointer....?

A] Screw thread mechanism

B] Quick Return mechanism

C] Rack and pinion mechanism

D] Hydraulic mechanism

INDUSTRIAL TRAINING INSTITUTE

Monthly Test-3, Marks- 20, Date:- ________________

(Every Question Carry Two Marks)

1-40] in following drawing, which of the front clearance angel?

A] Front clearance angle

B] Wedge angle

C] Cutting angle

D] Back rake angle

2-41] When cutting tool start his action & cutting force in increase at this position subsequent effect of tool is..?

A] Clearance angle of tool is high

B] Clearance angle of tool is low

C] Rake angle of tool is low

D] Rake angle of tool is high

3-42] The purpose of Rake angle for tool is?

A] Right direction for mental chips

B] Good finishing on job

C] For increase life of tool

D] For avoid friction in between job & tool

4-43] The purpose of provide clearance angle for cutting tool is?

A] For right direction of metal cutting chips

B] reduce friction on hit of job

C] for sage of job friction

D] for better finishing on job

5-44] If cutting tools setting upper centre height done what happen?

A] Encrease top Rake angle

B] less top Rake angle

C] No effect on Top Rake angle

D] Encrease clearance angle

6-45] What happen if cutting tool setting done lower of center height?

A] Encrease top Rake angle

B] Decrease top Rake angle

C] No any effect on to Rake

D] Decrease clearance angle

7-46] If cutting tool is upsetting of centre of job?

A] Encrease front clearance angle

B] Decrease front clearance angle

C] no any effect on front clearance angle

D] none of them

8-47] If cutting tool is down setting of centre of job?

A] Front clearance angle is increase

B] Front clearance angle is decrease

C] No any effect on clearance angle

D] None of them

9-48] Zero Rake angle give for tool?

A] To avoid friction of tool

B] For increase tool life

C] For increase straight of tool

D] For better finishing on job

10-49] For carbide tip tool turning on hard material it has.....ecential?

A] Side Rake angle

B] Zero Rake angle

C] Positive Rake angle

D] Negative Rake angle

INDUSTRIAL TRAINING INSTITUTE

Monthly Test-4, Marks- 20, Date:- _______________

(Every Question Carry Two Marks)

1-60] jig has tolerance..?

A] five present of job tolerance

B] ten percent of job tolerance

C] 20% to 50% of job tolerance

D] 100% of job tolerance

2-61] Following which jig is use for location from bore?

A] plate jig

B] solid jig

C] post jig

D] box jig

3-62] Following which jig having drill plate?

A] solid jig

B] plate jig

C] box jig

D] table jig

4-63] Following which locator is used for internal diameter location?

A] solid saports

B] Pin type locator

C] Vee locator

D] nest locator

5-64] Drm jig bushing-are generally hardened to -----------]

A] Mild steel

B] Cast iron

C] Cast steel

D] Tooi steel

6-65] Jigs is device which -------------

A] Locate the work piece

B] Holding and supporting the work piece

C] Guide the cutting tool

D] Does all the above

7-66] Which among the following jigs is used forllocation from a bore?

A] Plate jig

B] Solid jig

C] Post jig

D] Box jig

8-67] Fixture is a production device which -----------]

A] Holds and locate the work piece

B] Holds the piece

C] Chats the work piece,

D] Neither holds nor] Locates the-work piece

9-68] Which one of the following is used to guide tool and hold the job in mass production? '

A] Gauge]

B] Housing

C] Fixture

D] Jig

10-69] Which among the following is the purpose for proi/iding bushing in a drill jig?

A] For locating accurately and guiding the drill for precise drilling operation

B] For determining the size of the hole to be drilled

C] For easy drilling

D] For getting good finished surface in the drilled holes

INDUSTRIAL TRAINING INSTITUTE

Monthly Test-5, Marks- 20, Date:- _______________

(Every Question Carry Two Marks)

1-90] Centre line of the contact rollers and datum surface if the sine bar are

A] Same line' '

B] Parallel

C] Inclined

D] Perpendicular

2-91] The sine bar is made of -.

A] High carbon steel

B] Stabilized chromium steel '

C] High speed steel

D] Nicked steel

3-92] A sine bar with a length of l=200mm is used to check accurately the angle of a Work piece] The angle to be checked: 250 calculate the height 'h' of the slip gauges?

A] 84.54mm

B] 83.52mm

C] 81.81mm

D] 85.52mm

4-93] Which of the following statement is correct?'

A] Gauges are used to check the size

B] Template are used to chuck-the size

C] Gauges are used to measure the size

D] Gauges are used to check shape of component

5-94] At what standard temperature are the gauges kept in the section?

A] 100 C

B] 20° C

C] 100 F

D] 20° F

6-95] Which grade of slip gauge is generally used in workshop?

A] Grade 0

B] Grade l

C] Grade H

D] Grade 0

7-96] As per Indian Standards a special set gauge is used consisting of

A] 81 Pieces

B] 112 Pieces

C] 120 Pieces

D] 130 Pieces

8-97] The accuracy of reference gauge is

A] 0.05 mm

B] 0.01 mm

C] 0.001]

D] 0.0001 mm

9-98] In case of ant burr on slip gauge, it should be removed by

A] Filling

B] Lapping

C] Scraping

D] Grinding

10-99] Hardness of slip gauge should be?

A] More than 63 HRC

B] 58 HRC

C] 55 HRC

D] 50 HRC

INDUSTRIAL TRAINING INSTITUTE

Monthly Test-6, Marks- 20, Date:- _______________

(Every Question Carry Two Marks)

1-120] The cutting speed for brass with a H.S.S] tool is

A] 10 m/min

B] 25 m/min

C] 70 m/min

D] 140 m/min

2-121] The distance, which the cutting edge of a tool passes over the material in a minute while machining is Know as...

A] RPM

B] Feed

C] Machine speed

D] Cutting speed

3-122] The depth of cut for M24 x 3 mm internal thread is

A] 0.5412 x 3

B] 0.6134 x 3

C] 0.5 x 3

D] 0.7 x 3

4-123] To cut 24 x 3 mm internal acme threads, the core diameter of the job is

A] 20.00 mm

B] 21.66 mm

C] 21.00 mm

D] 20.60 mm

5-124] The depth of cut for metric square threading is

A] 0.6 x P

B] 0.5 x P

C] 0.5412 x P

D] 0.6412 x P

6-125] To cut buttress thread, the depth of cut is

A] 0.5412 x P

B] 0.6 x P

C] 0.7 x P

D] 0.75 x P

7-126] Lubricant is necessary to ....]

A] run the machine smoothly taking least load

B] Run the machine quickly

C] Stop the machine immediately

D] Produce work piece of greater accuracy

8-127] Extreme pressure additive (EPA] is mixed with cutting fluid for improving its power of.

A] Cooling

B] Lubrication

D] Production of the machined surface

C] Cleaning of cutting zone

9-128] The main purpose for using a lubricant in machine tools is to ------

A] Cool down the making parts

B] Prevent machine tool from heating

C] Wet the making parts for close contact

D] Minimize the friction between the making parts

10-129] Preventive maintenance is ....]

A] The maintenance involves the use of sensitive instruments

B] The maintenance generally performed by operator himself

C] The work carried only when machine break down

D] plan to minimize the unforeseen break down

INDUSTRIAL TRAINING INSTITUTE

Monthly Test-7, Marks- 20, Date:- _______________

(Every Question Carry Two Marks)

1-140] The number of threads per inch can be checked with a

A] tool gauge

B] metric rule by counting

C] ring gauge

D] screw pitch gauge

2-141] Which gauge is used to check the threading tool of lathe, for accuracy on the 60° angle?

A] Screw pitch gauge

B] Thread plug gauge

C] Centre gauge

D] Thread ring gauge

3-142] Tool maker's buttons are used to

A] adjust the slackness in the guide ways oi crossslide

B] alter the tool height

C] align the work for boring to a given datum

D] none of the above]

4-143] The space clearance between bore and screw is provided

A] for shifting the button position

B] for easy change of button

C] for lubricating bush

D] for easy clamping of button]

5-144] Normally button boring operations on irregular shaped heavy jobs are carried out in

A] three jaw chuck(universal]

B] faceplate

C] between centres

D] four jaw independent chuck]

6-145] Tool maker's buttons are made ot]

A] plastic

B] cast iron

C] hardened steel

D] bronze]

7-146] The smallest inside micrometer has the graduation marked on the sleeve

A] 10mm

B] 12mm

C] 13mm

D] 25mm

8-147] The method used to out multiple start thread is

A] forward and reverse switch method

B] use half nut method]

C] face plate and indexing drive plate method

D] attachment method]

9-148] Multiple start threads are used on

A] vice spindle

B] lathe Spindle

C] standard nut

D] pen cover]

10-149] Balancing is done in the face plate work

A] to increase the speed

B] to reduce the pressure on the tool

C] for uniform rotation of work

D] to get a good finish

INDUSTRIAL TRAINING INSTITUTE

Monthly Test-8, Marks- 20, Date:- _______________

(Every Question Carry Two Marks)

1-170] This bearings from the following are] Made in two halves and assembled in special Plummer blocks?

(A] Solid bearing

(B] Bearing

(C] Spit bearing

(D] Adjustable lid bearing

2-171] Which among the following type of bearing has a spherical bore on its race?

(A] Angular contact ball bearing

(B] Self aligning ball bearing

(C] Roller bearing

(D] Thrush ball bearing

3-172] What is the reason of reducing friction in roller bearing?

(A] Contact area

(B] Grease

(C] sites

4-173] It is necessary to have the Outside diameter of the bearing severally restricted due to limited bearing space in housing Select the bearing.

(A] Ball bearing

(B] Roller bearing

(C] Needle bearing

(D] Any of the above

5-174] Name of the bearing which have barrel shaped rollers and spherical bores in the outer race?

(A] Self aligning roller bearings

(B] Roller bearing

(C] Roller bearing

(D] Needle bearing

6-175] The material of races and rolling elements of anti-fliction bearing ....]

(A] Chromium steel or Chrome-nickel steel]

(B] Stainless steel]

(C] Cast iron]

(D] Bronze

7-176] When the anti-friction bearing is mounted right into the shaft] Pressure should be applied on this part.......]

(A] Inner race

(B] Outer race

(C] Cage

(D] Rolling elements

8-177] The heating temperature of bearing in -oil bath or induction heating process]

(A] (50°C to 90°C

(B] 90°C to 100°C

(C] 90°C to 120°C

(D] 90°C to 150°C

9-178] Rolling contact bearing should not be heated more than temperature]

A] 100°C

B] 120°C

C] 140°C

D] 150°C

10-179] Which among the following bearing material has a low load carting capacity?

(A] Cadmium based alloy

(B] White metal

(C] Lead bronze

(D] Cast iron

INDUSTRIAL TRAINING INSTITUTE

Monthly Test-9, Marks- 20, Date:- _______________

(Every Question Carry Two Marks)

1-238] The process of heating and cooling to change the structure of steel for obtaining the required properties is called

A] Hardening

B] Normalizing

C] Heat treatment

D] Tempering

2-239] The main purpose of annealing is to

A] Increase the hardness

B] Increase the toughness

C] Improve machinability

D] Improve distortion

3-240] The purpose of normalizing steel is to -----------

A] Remove the induced Stress

B] Improve genes and reduce brittleness

C] Soften the metal

D] Increase the surface?

4-241] Which one of the following process is used for hardenmg the outer 5" Annealing

A] Hardening

B] Tempering

C] Case Hardening

D] Tear surface

5-242] The purpose of producmg a component with tough and ductIle core and hard ou is known as.....]

A] Hardening

B] Case hardening

C] Tempering

D] annealing

6-243] Lower critical temperature of high carbon steel while hardening is ----------

A] 9600C

B] 900°C

c] 7230 c

D] 56O C

7-244] The process of Changing the structure and thus changing the properties by heating and 'cooling is known as --

A] Heat treatment

B] Alloying

C] Tempering

D] None of these

8-245] For refining the grain structure which one of the following heat treatment processes 'Is adopted]

A] Annealing

B] Hardening

C] Tempering

D] Normalising

9-246] Annealing is performed on iron and steel ---------

A] To remove internal stresses

B] To reduce hardness

C] To improve machinability

D] All of these

10-247] Which one of the following does not fall under the stages of heat treatment?

A] Heating

B] Cleaning

C] Quenching

D] Soaking

INDUSTRIAL TRAINING INSTITUTE

Monthly Test-10, Marks- 20, Date:- ________________

(Every Question Carry Two Marks)

1-257] In zero offset program indicates........... Code of following

A] X y z

B] X0 y0 z00

C] X10 Y20 Z30

D] G71

2-258] Work zero is......

A] Datum of machine zero on job position.

B] Indicate by X0Y0Z0.

C] Selection of point on job according to program.

D] The end of machining point

3-259] M command is used for starting operation and complete revolution cycle M03 means.

A] Stop the program.

B] Program completed and reset.

C] Complete the program.

D] Spindle clockwise motion

4-260] CNC machine is not manually operated it is control by...........

A] Program

B] operation

C] Cam

D] Plug board system

5-261] In CNC machine M13 means

A] coolant stop

B] coolant on

C] spindle stop

D] coolant on & spindle on

6-262] The function of power pack in CNC machine.

A] For balancing of lubricants heat.

B] For increasing heat of lubricants.

C] For destroy heat of lubricant.

D] Above all.

7-263] The section of CNC machine bed is.....

A] Flat

B] Half round

C] Rectangular

D] Triangular

8-264] Following which statement is disadvantage of CNC machine.

A] Less inspection charge.

B] Less tooling charge.

C] Increase production rate.

D] High establishment charge.

9-265] The point to point system is more effective for......

A] Turning

B] Profile milling

C] Grinding

D] Drilling

10-266] Tool setting on NC machine on...... unit.

A] Presetting device.

B] Order special device without machine.

C] On n c machine other empty time.

D] When other operation working on machine.

INDUSTRIAL TRAINING INSTITUTE

Monthly Test-11, Marks- 20, Date:- ________________

(Every Question Carry Two Marks)

1-281] Zero offset is the distance between.......... And..........

A] G41 & g42

B] Machine zero & work zero

C] Reference point and tapping mode

D] None of them

**2-282] The feed rate is programmed as mm per minute with G ....
And mm per- Revolution with G........**

A] G41 & g42

B] G 43 and G 40

C] G 94 and g95

D] None of them

3-283] For collection all instructions from....... In CNC control unit

A] Memory

B] Tape reader

C] Control panel

D] Operator

**4-284] For control forward and backward of- CNC drilling machine y
axis.........**

A] Spindle

B] Table

C] Clockwise

D] Column

5-285] M 01 command means.....

A] For stopping programs

B] End of program and reset

C] Stopping programs condition

D] Clockwise rotation of machine spindle

6-286] CNC machine is founded by American scientist john person in....... Year

A] 1950

B] 1952

C] 1955

D] 1957

7-287] Name of unit used to command the CNC machine.

A] Control unit

B] Memory unit

C] Input unit

D] Output unit

8-288] Name of unit used to processing the data in CNC machine.

A] Memory unit

B] Control unit

C] Input unit

D] Output unit

9-289] Name of unit used to storing the data in CNC machine.

A] Input unit

B] Control unit

C] Memory unit

D] Output unit

10-290] Name of unit used to calculation of data in CNC machine.

A] Output unit

B] Arithmetic unit

C] Memory unit

D] Input unit

INDUSTRIAL TRAINING INSTITUTE

Monthly Test-12, Marks- 20, Date:- _______________

(Every Question Carry Two Marks)

1-308] In CNC program which letter is used to indicate the sequence number of the block

A] N

B] G

C] F

D] S

2-309] In CNC program which letter is used to indicate position of linear axis

A] ABC

B] UVW

C] XYZ

D] IJK

3-310] One of the below letters used in CNC program for Feed rate

A] S

B] F

C] T

D] M

4-311] One of the below letters used in CNC program for spindle speed in RPM

A] M

B] T

C] S

D] F

5-312] In CNC program which letter is used to indicate TOOL function number of tool

A] T

B] S

C] M

D] F

6-313] In CNC program which miscellaneous function used to program stop

A] M03

B] M00

C] M01

D] M02

7-314] One of the below miscellaneous function used to program optional Stop

A] M 01

B] M 02

C] M 03

D] M 04

8-315] In CNC program miscellaneous function M02 is used to......

A] Program stop

B] Optional program stop

C] End of program

D] Clockwise spindle on

9-316] In CNC program miscellaneous function M03 is used to..........

A] Counter clockwise spindle on

B] Clockwise spindle on

C] Spindle off

D] Tool change

10-317] One of the below miscellaneous function used in CNC program for spindle stop.

A] M04

B] M05

C] M06

D] M07